Mortgage And Interest Rates

What you should know to get a risk free deal

By

Bert Rivers

Table of contents

Introduction

Mortgages and interest rates are two of the most important financial concepts that anyone buying a home will need to understand. A mortgage is a loan that allows you to buy a property, and the interest rate is the cost of borrowing that money.

For most people, buying a home is the biggest financial commitment they will ever make. A mortgage can be a daunting prospect, but it's important to remember that it's just a loan. Like any loan, it has to be repaid, with interest.

The interest rate you pay on your mortgage will have a significant impact on your monthly repayments. A higher interest rate means higher monthly repayments, while a lower interest rate means lower monthly repayments.

Interest rates are set by lenders, and they can fluctuate depending on a number of factors, such as the state of the economy and the Bank of England's base rate.

It's important to shop around for the best mortgage deal possible. A small difference in interest rates can make a big difference to your monthly repayments over the lifetime of your mortgage.

In this book, we will explain everything you need to know about mortgages and interest rates. We will cover topics such as:

- The different types of mortgages available
- How mortgage rates are calculated
- The factors that affect mortgage affordability
- The mortgage application process

- How to choose the right mortgage
- How to manage your mortgage
- The impact of mortgages on your overall finances

We will also provide you with tips on how to get the best possible mortgage deal.

By the end of this book, you will have a comprehensive understanding of mortgages and interest rates. You will be able to make informed decisions about your mortgage and choose the right deal for your needs.

So, let's get started!

Chapter 1

Understanding mortgages in the UK

Types of mortgages available in the UK

There are two main types of mortgages available in the UK: fixed-rate mortgages and variable-rate mortgages.

Fixed-rate mortgages offer a fixed interest rate for a set period of time, typically 2-5 years. This denotes that your monthly pay will remain the same for the duration of the fixed-rate period, regardless of changes in the overall interest rate environment. Fixed-rate mortgages can be a good option for borrowers who want predictability in their monthly payments.

Variable-rate mortgages have an interest rate that can change over time, typically based on a benchmark interest rate, such as the Bank of England base rate. This denotes that your monthly pay could go up or down over time. Variable-rate mortgages can be a good option for borrowers who are comfortable with the risk of fluctuating interest rates.

In addition to fixed-rate and variable-rate mortgages, there are a number of other types of mortgages available in the UK, including:

- **Tracker mortgages:** Tracker mortgages have a variable interest rate that is linked to a benchmark interest rate, such as the Bank of England base rate. However, tracker mortgages typically have a lower margin than standard variable-rate mortgages, meaning that your interest rate will be closer to the benchmark rate.

- **Discount mortgages:** Discount mortgages offer a discounted interest rate for a set period of time, typically 2-5 years. This means that your interest rate will be lower than the lender's standard variable rate for the duration of the discount period.

- **Offset mortgages:** Offset mortgages allow you to link your savings account to your mortgage account. This means that your savings will offset the balance of your mortgage, reducing the amount of interest you pay.

- **Buy-to-let mortgages:** Buy-to-let mortgages are designed for borrowers who are purchasing a property to rent out. Buy-to-let mortgages typically have higher interest rates and shorter loan terms than residential mortgages.

- **Help to Buy mortgages**: Help to Buy mortgages are government-backed mortgages that can help first-time buyers and certain other borrowers to purchase a property with a smaller deposit.

Ways in choosing the right mortgage for you

When choosing a mortgage, it is important to consider your individual needs and financial situation. Factors to consider include:

- **Your financial budget:** How much can you afford to pay in monthly mortgage payments?

- **Your loan term**: How long do you want to repay your mortgage?

- **Your interest rate**: What interest rate are you comfortable with?

- **Your risk tolerance:** How comfortable are you with the risk of fluctuating interest rates?

- **Your needs:** What type of mortgage is right for your needs, such as a buy-to-let mortgage or a Help to Buy mortgage?

It is also important to compare offers from multiple lenders before choosing a mortgage. This will help you to get the best possible interest rate and terms.

Conclusion

There are a variety of mortgages available in the UK, each with its own advantages and disadvantages. It is important to choose the right mortgage for your individual needs and financial situation. Make sure to assess mortgage offers from several lenders before making your selection

Choosing the right Mortgage for you

Mortgage rates in the UK are determined by lenders, considering various factors, such as:

1. The Bank of England base rate, which lenders typically adjust by adding a margin to set their mortgage rates.

2. The loan-to-value ratio (LTV), with lower LTVs receiving more favorable interest rates due to lower perceived risk.

3. Borrower's credit history, with better credit leading to lower interest rates.

4. The length of the loan term, where longer terms often come with higher rates than shorter ones.

A simplified example of mortgage rate calculation is as follows:

Example:

- Loan amount: £200,000
- Property value: £300,000
- LTV: 66.7%
- Bank of England base rate: 2.25%
- Lender's margin: 1.5%
- Mortgage rate calculation: Bank of England base rate + lender's margin = mortgage rate
- 2.25% + 1.5% = 3.75%

In this example, the borrower would receive a 3.75% mortgage rate. Note that rates can vary between lenders, even for borrowers with similar credit histories and LTVs. It's crucial to compare offers from multiple lenders when selecting a mortgage.

Additional factors affecting mortgage rates include the state of the economy, supply and demand for mortgages, and government policies like the Help to Buy scheme. To secure the best mortgage rate:

1. Compare offers from multiple lenders to ensure the best rate.
2. Improve your financial situation, including your credit score and LTV.
3. Consider using a mortgage broker for expert assistance in finding the ideal mortgage for your needs.

Factors affecting mortgage affordability

Mortgage affordability refers to your capacity to comfortably meet your monthly mortgage payments, while also addressing existing debts, household expenses, and living costs. Several factors impact mortgage affordability, including:

1. Income: Lenders evaluate your debt-to-income ratio (DTI), where a DTI of 36% or less is typically seen as affordable.

2. Debt: Total debt-to-income ratio (TDTI) considers all monthly debt payments, including the mortgage, with a DTI of 43% or less often deemed affordable.

3. Down payment: A larger down payment reduces the amount you need to borrow, lowering monthly payments.

4. Interest rate: Lower rates lead to more manageable monthly payments.

5. Property price: The cost of the property affects affordability; pricier homes require larger mortgages and higher payments.

Other factors influencing affordability encompass job stability, credit history, and living expenses. It's crucial to demonstrate consistent income, a good credit history, and the ability to cover both mortgage payments and living costs.

To enhance mortgage affordability:

1. Boost your income through raises, side gigs, or second jobs.

2. Reduce debt by paying it off, consolidating at lower rates, or using zero-interest credit cards.

3. Save for a larger down payment to reduce borrowing needs.

4. Obtain pre-approval to determine borrowing limits and monthly payments, aiding in budgeting.

5. Compare offers from multiple lenders for the best interest rate.

Assess your lifestyle and spending habits; consider cutting back on discretionary expenses like dining out and entertainment if needed to make your mortgage affordable. Mortgage affordability is influenced by numerous factors, and consulting a financial advisor for personalized guidance is advisable if you encounter challenges.

The mortgage application process

The mortgage application procedure can differ among lenders, but there are general steps common to all applications:

Step 1: Obtain Pre-approval

Start by getting pre-approved for a mortgage, which provides an estimate of your borrowing capacity and monthly payments. To secure pre-approval, you must furnish basic financial information, such as income, debt, and employment status, to the lender.

Step 2: Property Search

Following pre-approval, you can begin searching for a property to purchase. When you identify a property of interest, you'll need to make an offer. If your offer is accepted, you'll proceed to sign a purchase agreement.

Step 3: Formal Mortgage Application

Upon signing the purchase agreement, you'll need to submit a formal mortgage application to your chosen lender. This application necessitates more comprehensive financial details and property-related information.

Step 4: Underwriting

Once you've submitted your mortgage application, the lender initiates the underwriting process. This phase entails verifying your information and evaluating your creditworthiness. The underwriting process may extend over several weeks.

Step 5: Loan Approval

If your loan is approved, the lender will issue a loan commitment letter outlining the loan terms, such as interest rate, loan duration, and monthly payments.

Step 6: Closing

The closing phase, the grand finale of the mortgage journey, is when you officially become a property owner by signing the mortgage documents.

To make this dream a reality, you'll need a set of documents for your mortgage application. While the specifics may vary between lenders, the usual suspects include proof of income (pay stubs or tax returns), proof of employment (that trusty employer's letter), proof of assets (bank or investment statements), evidence of debt (those credit card or loan statements), and a copy of your purchase agreement.

Now, let's sprinkle some success into your mortgage application journey:

1. Get pre-approved before embarking on your property hunt.
2. Polish up that credit score; it's your golden ticket.
3. Aim for a low debt-to-income ratio to win over lenders.
4. If you can, make a generous down payment.
5. Be ready with all the necessary paperwork; no missing ingredients allowed.

If the mortgage application recipe still seems complex, don't fret. Consult a financial advisor or a mortgage broker for expert guidance and a fortified application.

For first-time buyers, there's a treasury of government assistance schemes awaiting exploration. These programs are like a guardian angel for your homeownership dreams. Some popular ones include:

- Help to Buy: A government lifeline, offering equity loans up to 20% of the new home's price to ease the down payment burden.
- Lifetime ISA (LISA): A magical savings account that grants a 25% bonus on savings up to £4,000 per year, perfect for your first home or retirement.
- Right to Buy: This empowerment lets council or housing association tenants buy their home at a reduced price.
- Shared Ownership: A bridge to ownership, allowing you to own a share of a property (usually 25-75%) and gradually buy more.

- And that's not all; there are other programs like FHA, USDA, and VA loans, each with its unique benefits.

To uncover the treasure trove of government assistance, contact your local housing authority or visit the HUD website. Alternatively, embark on a digital quest by searching for "first-time homebuyer assistance programs" tailored to your state.

In a nutshell, with the right mix of research and determination, you can unlock the door to homeownership with these government programs tailored to first-time buyers. Your goal of owning a house is close.

Chapter 2

Interest rates and the UK economy

The Bank of England and Its Role in Interest Rate Management

- **What is the Bank of England?**

The Bank of England functions as the United Kingdom's central bank and plays a crucial role in shaping the nation's economic policies.

- **What are interest rates?**

Interest rates signify the expense associated with borrowing money and are decided upon by banks and financial institutions.

The Bank of England's monetary policy significantly influences these rates.

- **Why does the Bank of England establish interest rates?**

The Bank of England administers interest rates to achieve two principal goals:

1. Maintaining low and consistent inflation: Inflation gauges the rate at which prices elevate over time, and the Bank of England's objective is to uphold inflation at 2%.

2. Upholding financial stability: The Bank of England strives to guarantee a stable financial system capable of sustaining economic growth.

- How does the Bank of England regulate interest rates?

The Bank of England employs its Monetary Policy Committee (MPC), which convenes eight times annually to determine interest rates. The MPC evaluates a variety of economic indicators, including inflation, economic growth, and unemployment, when making its decisions.

- The impact of interest rates on the economy

Low interest rates translate to more affordable borrowing, encouraging businesses to invest and consumers to increase spending, thereby stimulating economic growth. However, they may also trigger inflation due to heightened consumer spending.

Conversely, high interest rates can deter borrowing, potentially slowing economic growth. On the positive side, they can aid in curbing inflation by limiting consumer spending.

- Utilizing Your Knowledge of Interest Rates

Understanding interest rates can help you make more informed financial decisions. For instance, if you are contemplating a loan, like a mortgage or business loan, it is vital to compare interest rates from different lenders.

Moreover, your understanding of interest rates can guide your investment choices. When considering investments in bonds, it's essential to factor in the current interest rate environment.

- In Conclusion

The Bank of England's responsibility in establishing interest rates is paramount. Given the profound impact of interest rates on the economy, it is essential to grasp their mechanics and determination.

Here are some actionable suggestions for implementing this information:

1. Before borrowing money, compare interest rates offered by different lenders.

2. When making investment decisions, consider the prevailing interest rate conditions.

3. Be aware that alterations in interest rates can influence your financial situation, both positively and negatively.

How Interest Rates Affect Mortgages

Forecasting future interest rates

Predicting future interest rates is an intricate endeavor, yet it holds significant importance for businesses, investors, and homeowners, necessitating a grasp of the factors that exert an influence.

- Determinants of Interest Rates

Numerous elements can shape interest rates:

1. Economic Growth: Robust economic growth usually prompts central banks to heighten interest rates, aiming to avert excessive inflation.

2. Inflation: Elevated inflation frequently results in central banks raising interest rates to curtail economic growth and subdue inflation.

3. Unemployment: Central banks are often hesitant to elevate interest rates when unemployment levels are high, as doing so could further impede economic growth and escalate job losses.

4. Government Debt: Concerns about excessive government debt can also prompt central banks to boost interest rates, as high debt levels carry inflation risks.

- Forecasting Techniques

Economists employ a variety of models for projecting future interest rates, considering the aforementioned factors along with other economic indicators.

The Taylor rule, a prevalent forecasting model, utilizes a straightforward equation that predicts interest rates based on inflation and the output gap, the difference between the actual and potential economic output.

Another widely used forecasting model is the term structure model, which forecasts interest rates based on yields of government bonds with varying maturities.

- Challenges and Considerations

Anticipating future interest rates is arduous due to the intricacies of predicting the future economic landscape. Furthermore, central banks can enact unexpected alterations in monetary policy, adding to the complexity of accurate interest rate forecasts.

- Leveraging Interest Rate Forecasts

Interest rate projections serve as valuable tools for making sound financial choices. Businesses can utilize these forecasts to formulate capital expenditure plans, investors can make informed investment decisions, and homeowners can determine whether to opt for a fixed-rate or variable-rate mortgage.

- In Conclusion

Anticipating future interest rates, while challenging, is crucial for businesses, investors, and homeowners, necessitating a comprehensive understanding of the influential factors. Interest rate forecasts empower better financial decisions.

Consider these pointers when using interest rate forecasts:

1. Acknowledge the inherent limitations of interest rate forecasts. No forecasting model is infallible, and interest rates can change unexpectedly.

2. Combine interest rate forecasts with other economic indicators for a more comprehensive economic assessment.

3. Factor in your business or household's risk tolerance when making financial decisions guided by interest rate forecasts.

The Intricate Interplay of Interest Rates and Real Estate Values

Interest rates and house prices rank among the most pivotal economic variables for both households and businesses. Interest rates influence the cost of borrowing money, which, in turn, can impact the demand for housing. Conversely, house prices can have repercussions on the overall economic well-being.

- Theoretical Framework

The connection between interest rates and house prices can be elucidated through the following theoretical framework:

1. Demand for Housing: Housing demand hinges on several factors, including income, population growth, and interest rates. Lower

interest rates translate to more affordable borrowing for home purchases, thereby increasing the demand for housing.

2. Supply of Housing: The housing supply is influenced by various factors, such as land costs, labor, and materials. In the short term, housing supply is typically inelastic, meaning it does not fluctuate significantly in response to price changes.

3. Equilibrium Price: The equilibrium price of housing materializes when housing demand aligns with housing supply.

- Empirical Evidence

Extensive empirical research supports the inverse relationship between interest rates and house prices. Studies indicate that lower interest rates correspond to higher house prices, and conversely, higher interest rates tend to result in lower house prices. For instance, research by the Federal Reserve Bank of St. Louis reveals that a 1% decrease in interest rates leads to a 6% increase in house prices. Meanwhile, a study from the National Bureau of Economic Research found that a 1% increase in interest rates leads to a 3% decrease in house prices.

- Policy Implications

The association between interest rates and house prices carries significant policy implications. Central banks, like the Federal Reserve, employ interest rates as a tool for economic management. In times of elevated inflation, the Fed typically raises interest rates, which can decelerate economic growth and mitigate house prices. Conversely, during periods of low inflation, the Fed often lowers interest rates, which can stimulate economic growth and elevate house prices.

- Conclusion

The interplay between interest rates and house prices is multifaceted, yet extensive empirical research supports the inverse relationship between these variables. Central banks employ interest rates to regulate the economy, and this relationship's implications extend to households and businesses.

Additional Considerations

- Additional Factors Affecting House Prices: Besides interest rates, various other factors can influence house prices, including the overall economy, job market conditions, and credit availability.

- Regional Variations: The link between interest rates and house prices can exhibit regional disparities, primarily due to varying housing markets and economic situations.

- Long-Term Trends: Over the long haul, house prices tend to ascend. This trend is driven by factors like population growth and economic expansion.

Real-Life Examples

- The 2008 Housing Crisis: The 2008 housing crisis provides a notable illustration of the interplay between interest rates and house prices. Preceding the crisis, the Federal Reserve maintained low interest rates to stimulate the economy, causing a housing market boom. Nonetheless, when the Fed initiated interest rate hikes in 2004, the housing market cooled, ultimately leading to a decline in house prices and contributing to the 2008 financial crisis.

- The COVID-19 Pandemic: The COVID-19 pandemic significantly impacted interest rates and house prices. In response to the pandemic, the Federal Reserve lowered interest rates to near-zero levels. This spurred a surge in housing demand as more individuals could afford to purchase homes. Consequently, house prices saw substantial growth in 2020 and 2021. However, in 2022, the Fed commenced raising interest rates to combat inflation, leading to reduced housing demand and a deceleration in house price growth.

Chapter 3

Choosing the right mortgage

Fixed-rate vs. variable-rate mortgages.

Fixed-Rate Mortgages:
- Interest rate remains constant throughout the mortgage term.
- Monthly payments are predictable and don't change.

- Offers lower risk as you're shielded from interest rate increases.

Variable-Rate Mortgages:

- Interest rates can fluctuate over time.

- Monthly payments can change with adjustments based on a benchmark interest rate.

- Carries a higher risk of interest rate increases but can save you money if rates go down.

Selecting the ideal mortgage hinges on your unique circumstances:

- Financial Situation: Assess your budget, job stability, income, and existing debts.

- Risk Tolerance: Decide if you're comfortable with potential payment fluctuations due to interest rate changes.

- Future Plans: Consider the duration you intend to stay in your home.

Remember that fixed-rate mortgages often have higher initial rates due to lenders assuming more risk. Variable rates can be advantageous if you anticipate interest rates decreasing but come with the risk of rate hikes. Be aware that both types may have prepayment penalties.

If you're uncertain, consulting a mortgage broker is advisable. They can evaluate your situation and recommend the best mortgage type. Your final choice should align with your financial goals and individual circumstances.

Tracker mortgages vs. discount mortgages

Tracker mortgages and discount mortgages are two types of variable-rate mortgages that are popular in the UK. Both types of mortgages have their own advantages and disadvantages, so it is important to compare them carefully before choosing one.

Tracker mortgages

Tracker mortgages track the Bank of England base rate, which is the rate at which banks can borrow money from the central bank. This means that the interest rate on a tracker mortgage will go up or down whenever the base rate changes.

Tracker mortgages typically have lower interest rates than other types of mortgages, such as standard variable rate (SVR) mortgages. This is because the Bank of England base rate is usually quite low. However, it is important to note that the interest rate on a tracker mortgage can go up as well as down.

Advantages of tracker mortgages:

- Interest rates in this category are notably more modest compared to alternative mortgage options.
- Flexible, as the interest rate can be changed to reflect changes in the base rate

Disadvantages of tracker mortgages:

- Interest rates possess the capacity to ascend just as readily as they can descend.
- May not be suitable for borrowers who need certainty about their monthly repayments

Discount mortgages

Discount mortgages offer a discounted interest rate below the lender's standard variable rate (SVR). This means that the interest rate on a discount mortgage will be lower than the SVR for a certain period of time, usually two to five years.

After the initial discount period ends, the interest rate on a discount mortgage will revert to the lender's SVR. Discount mortgages can be a good option for borrowers who want to take advantage of lower interest rates in the short term, but who also want some certainty about their monthly repayments in the future.

Advantages of discount mortgages:

- Lower interest rates than the lender's SVR for a certain period of time
- More certainty about monthly repayments than tracker mortgages

Disadvantages of discount mortgages:

- Interest rates will revert to the lender's SVR after the initial discount period ends

- May not be as competitive as tracker mortgages in the long term

Which type of mortgage is right for you?

The best type of mortgage for you will depend on your individual circumstances and preferences. If you are comfortable with the risk of interest rates going up, and you want to take advantage of the lowest possible interest rates, then a tracker mortgage may be a good option for you.

If you need more certainty about your monthly repayments, or if you think that interest rates are likely to go up in the future, then a discount mortgage may be a better choice.

It is important to compare different mortgage deals from different lenders before choosing one. You should also consider your own financial situation and risk tolerance when making your decision.

Additional considerations

When choosing between a tracker mortgage and a discount mortgage, there are a few other things to keep in mind:

- Tracker mortgages may have an early repayment charge (ERC). This is a fee that you will have to pay if you repay your mortgage early. Discount mortgages typically do not have ERCs.

- Discount mortgages may have a higher SVR than tracker mortgages. This means that your interest rate could be higher after the initial discount period ends.

- Tracker mortgages may be more suitable for borrowers who plan to stay in their home for a long time. This is because you can benefit from lower interest rates for longer.

Discount mortgages may be more suitable for borrowers who plan to move house within a few years.

It is important to seek professional advice from a qualified mortgage advisor before choosing a mortgage. They can help you to compare different deals and choose the right one for your individual needs.

Offset mortgages vs. repayment mortgages

Offset mortgages

Offset mortgages are a type of mortgage where your savings are used to reduce the amount of your mortgage that you are charged interest on. This means that you can pay off your mortgage more quickly and save money on interest.

Offset mortgages work by linking your savings account to your mortgage account. The money in your savings account is offset against the balance of your mortgage, meaning that you only pay interest on the remaining amount.

For example, if you have a £200,000 mortgage and £50,000 in savings, you will only pay interest on £150,000. This is because your savings are offsetting £50,000 of your mortgage balance.

Advantages of offset mortgages:

* You can save money on interest Accelerating your mortgage repayment is within your reach.

- You have flexibility with your savings, as you can access them at any time

Disadvantages of offset mortgages:

- Interest rates on offset mortgages are typically higher than on repayment mortgages
- You need to have a significant amount of savings to benefit from an offset mortgage

Repayment mortgages

Repayment mortgages are the most common type of mortgage in the UK. With a repayment mortgage, you make fixed monthly repayments over the term of the mortgage. When the term reaches its conclusion, the mortgage shall be entirely settled.

Advantages of repayment mortgages:

- Fixed monthly repayments make it easier to budget

- You have certainty about your monthly repayments
- Repayment mortgages are more widely available than offset mortgages

Disadvantages of repayment mortgages:

- You will pay more interest over the lifetime of the mortgage than with an offset mortgage
- You may not be able to pay off your mortgage early without incurring an early repayment charge (ERC)

Which type of mortgage is right for you?

The best type of mortgage for you will depend on your individual circumstances and preferences. If you have a significant amount of savings and you want to save money on interest, then an offset mortgage may be a good option for you.

If you need more certainty about your monthly repayments or you do not have a lot of savings, then a repayment mortgage may be a better choice.

It is important to compare different mortgage deals from different lenders before choosing one. You should also consider your own financial situation and risk tolerance when making your decision.

Example

Here is an example of how an offset mortgage can save you money:

Repayment mortgage

- Mortgage amount: £200,000
- Interest rate: 3%
- Term: 25 years

Total interest paid: £112,699

Offset mortgage

- Mortgage amount: £200,000
- Interest rate: 3.5%

- Term: 25 years
- Savings balance: £50,000

Total interest paid: £97,083

As you can see, the offset mortgage saves the borrower £15,616 in interest over the lifetime of the mortgage.

Conclusion

Offset mortgages and repayment mortgages both have their own advantages and disadvantages. The best type of mortgage for you will depend on your individual circumstances and preferences. It is important to compare different mortgage deals from different lenders before choosing one and to seek professional advice from a qualified mortgage advisor.

Interest-only mortgages

An interest-only mortgage is a type of mortgage where the borrower only makes interest payments on the loan for a certain period of time, typically 5, 10, or 25 years. At the end of the interest-only period, the borrower must repay the entire principal amount of the loan in one lump sum.

Interest-only mortgages can be useful for borrowers who need to keep their monthly repayments low in the short term. For example, borrowers who are buying a property to renovate and sell on may choose to take out an interest-only mortgage so that they can keep their monthly repayments low while they are working on the property.

However, it is important to note that interest-only mortgages are riskier than other types of mortgages because the borrower is responsible for repaying the entire principal amount of the loan at the end of the interest-only period. If the borrower does not have a plan in place for repaying the principal, they could be forced to sell their property or refinance their mortgage at a higher interest rate.

How interest-only mortgages work

Interest-only mortgages are typically structured as adjustable-rate mortgages (ARMs), which means that the interest rate on the loan can change over time. The interest rate on an ARM is typically based on an index rate, such as the Bank of England base rate.

During the interest-only period, the borrower will make monthly payments that cover the interest on the loan. The principal amount of the loan will remain the same until the end of the interest-only period.

At the end of the interest-only period, the borrower must repay the entire principal amount of the loan in one lump sum. This can be done by selling the property, refinancing the mortgage, or using savings.

Advantages and disadvantages of interest-only mortgages

Advantages:

- Lower monthly repayments in the short term
- Can be useful for borrowers who need to keep their monthly repayments low
- Can be used to finance a wide range of purposes, such as buying a property to renovate and sell on

Disadvantages:

- Riskier than other types of mortgages because the borrower is responsible for repaying the entire principal amount of the loan at the end of the interest-only period

- Monthly repayments can increase if the interest rate on the loan goes up
- Borrowers must have a plan in place for repaying the principal amount of the loan at the end of the interest-only period

Who should consider an interest-only mortgage?

Interest-only mortgages might align with the preferences of borrowers who:

- Need to keep their monthly repayments low in the short term

  Do you have intentions to put your property on the market in the coming few years?

  Have a significant amount of savings that they can use to repay the principal amount of the loan at the end of the interest-only period

However, it is important to note that interest-only mortgages are not suitable for everyone. Borrowers should carefully consider their financial situation and risk tolerance before taking out an interest-only mortgage.

Tips for borrowers considering an interest-only mortgage

- Make sure you have a plan in place for repaying the principal amount of the loan at the end of the interest-only period.

- Consider taking out an interest-only mortgage for a shorter period of time, such as 5 or 10 years. This will give you more time to save up for the principal repayment.

- Get professional advice from a qualified mortgage advisor before taking out an interest-only mortgage.

Choosing a mortgage lender

Choosing a mortgage lender is one of the most important financial decisions you will ever make. The lender you choose should be able to offer you a mortgage product that meets your individual needs and circumstances, and they should be able to provide you with excellent customer service.

Here are a few tips on how to choose a mortgage lender:

1. Compare interest rates and fees from different lenders. Don't rush into an agreement with the initial lender you engage with. It's important to compare interest rates and fees from

different lenders before choosing one. You can use a mortgage comparison website to compare rates from different lenders in one place.

2. Consider the lender's reputation. It's important to choose a lender with a good reputation. You can check a lender's reputation by reading online reviews and talking to other borrowers. You can also check the Consumer Financial Protection Bureau (CFPB) website for complaints against lenders.

3. Make sure the lender is licensed and insured. All mortgage lenders must be licensed and insured. You can check a lender's license status with your state's banking department.

4. Ask about the lender's pre-approval process. Getting pre-approved for a

mortgage before you start shopping for a home is a good idea. This step provides a glimpse into your borrowing capacity and the anticipated monthly financial commitments. Ask the lender about their pre-approval process and what documentation you will need to provide.

5. Ask about the lender's closing costs. Closing costs are the fees that you will pay to close on your mortgage. Closing costs can vary depending on the lender and the type of mortgage you choose. Ask the lender about their closing costs upfront so that you can budget for them.

Once you have compared interest rates and fees, considered the lender's reputation, and made sure the lender is licensed and insured, you can start to narrow down your choices. At this point, it's important to talk to the lenders you're interested in and ask them questions about their products and services.

Here are a few questions you should ask potential mortgage lenders:

- What types of mortgage products do you offer?
- What are your interest rates and fees?
- What is your pre-approval process?
- What are your closing costs?
- What is your customer service policy?

It's also important to ask potential mortgage lenders about their experience with borrowers in your situation. For example, if you're a first-time homebuyer, you'll want to choose a lender who has experience working with first-time homebuyers.

Once you've asked all of your questions and compared the different lenders, you can choose the lender that you feel most comfortable with.

Here are a few additional tips on how to choose a mortgage lender:

- Get referrals from friends, family, and real estate professionals. People you know may be able to refer you to a mortgage lender that they had a good experience with.

- Work with a mortgage broker. A mortgage broker can help you compare mortgage products from different lenders.

- Don't be afraid to negotiate. Once you've found a lender that you're interested in, don't be afraid to negotiate the interest rate and fees. Choosing a mortgage lender is an important decision, but it doesn't have to be overwhelming. By following these tips, you can find the right lender for your needs.

Chapter 4

Managing your mortgage

Making mortgage repayments

Meeting your mortgage repayment obligations is a pivotal financial responsibility for countless individuals. Ensuring that you make your monthly mortgage payments in a timely and complete manner is essential to evade late fees and penalties.

Methods for Making Mortgage Repayments Several options are available for making mortgage repayments:

1. **Direct Debit**: Establish a direct debit from your bank account to your lender's account. This approach stands as the most convenient way to fulfill your mortgage payments, guaranteeing on-time, full payments each month.

2. **Manual Payment**: Initiate manual payments from your bank account to your lender's account, a process that can be executed online, by phone, or through traditional mail.

3. **In-Person Payment:** Visit a bank branch to make your mortgage payment.

Determining the Timing of Mortgage Repayments

The majority of mortgage repayments are typically due on the first day of each month. Nonetheless, certain lenders might offer alternative due dates, such as the 15th or 25th of the month. Verifying your lender's specific repayment schedule is essential.

Consequences of Missing a Mortgage Repayment

Should you fail to make a mortgage repayment, your lender will usually impose a late fee, the amount of which varies depending on the lender. Persistent non-payment may lead to further actions by your lender, including the possibility of home repossession.

Preventing Missed Mortgage Repayments

To mitigate the risk of missing mortgage repayments, consider these strategies:

1. Direct Debit Setup: Initiate a direct debit arrangement from your bank account to your lender's account.

2. Budget Management: Develop a comprehensive budget to ensure your account consistently contains the necessary funds to cover your monthly mortgage payment.

3. Set Reminders: Establish reminders on your electronic devices to keep track of your repayment due date.

If you encounter difficulties meeting your mortgage obligations, it is advisable to contact your lender at the earliest opportunity. They may offer assistance in finding a viable solution.

Suggestions for Mortgage Repayments

Here are some valuable suggestions for handling your mortgage repayments:

1. **Exceed Minimum Payments:** Consider making payments exceeding the minimum requirement. Doing so accelerates the mortgage payoff, resulting in interest savings.

2. **Explore Refinancing:** Should interest rates have decreased since your initial mortgage agreement, investigate the possibility of refinancing your mortgage. This action could lead to reduced monthly mortgage payments.

3. Lump Sum Payment: If you possess surplus funds, contemplate making a lump sum payment on your mortgage to decrease the principal balance and subsequently reduce monthly mortgage payments.

In Conclusion

Meeting your mortgage repayment responsibilities is of utmost importance. By heeding the advice above, you can effectively avoid missed repayments and potentially save on interest expenses.

Overpaying on your mortgage

Making additional payments on your mortgage, often referred to as overpaying, involves contributing more than the minimum required monthly payment. Engaging in this practice offers several advantages, such as:

1. Reducing Interest Payments: Overpaying on your mortgage lowers the principal balance, ultimately resulting in reduced interest payments over the life of the loan.

2. Accelerated Mortgage Payoff: Overpayments can expedite the repayment of your mortgage compared to the original schedule. This not only saves you a substantial amount of interest but also grants you the comfort of a debt-free status.

3. Enhancing Credit Score: Consistently making overpayments showcases your responsible borrowing behavior to lenders. It demonstrates your ability to exceed minimum debt payments, which can contribute to an improved credit score.

Ways to Overpay on Your Mortgage

You have multiple options for making overpayments on your mortgage:

1. Lump Sum Payment: You can make a one-time, substantial lump sum payment.

2. Increase Monthly Payment: Adjust your regular monthly mortgage payment to a higher amount.

3. Additional Payments: Make extra payments throughout the year, beyond the standard monthly requirement.

Determining the Ideal Overpayment Amount

The suitable amount to overpay on your mortgage hinges on your specific financial circumstances and objectives. While a significant lump sum payment can drastically reduce interest and the mortgage term, even smaller, regular overpayments accumulate over time, leading to long-term savings.

Commencing Your Overpayments

The sooner you embark on your overpayment journey, the greater the financial benefits. Nevertheless, it's never too late to begin making overpayments. Even if you only have a few years left on your mortgage, overpaying can still yield interest savings.

Overpayment Limits

Lenders often impose annual limits on the extent of overpayments you can make. These limits are typically expressed as a percentage of the initial principal balance. For example, a lender might permit overpayments up to 10% of the original principal balance each year.

Potential Drawbacks of Overpaying

Overpaying on your mortgage involves tying up your funds in your home. This may limit access to the money for unforeseen emergencies. Furthermore, if you sell your home before fully paying off the mortgage, you won't be able to recover the funds you've overpaid.

In Conclusion

Overpaying on your mortgage is a commendable method to save on interest and achieve faster mortgage repayment. However, it's crucial to carefully evaluate the pros and cons before committing to overpayments. If you're contemplating overpaying your mortgage, consulting a financial advisor to align your decision with your individual financial situation and goals is advisable.

Remortgaging

Remortgaging involves the process of transitioning from your current mortgage to a new one, whether with your existing lender or a different one. This practice is undertaken for various reasons, including securing a more favorable interest rate, adjusting mortgage terms, or accessing equity.

How Remortgaging Works

When you decide to remortgage, you'll be required to settle the remaining balance of your current mortgage and then initiate a new mortgage for the same amount or less. The new mortgage comes with modified terms and conditions, encompassing alterations in the interest rate, repayment period, and associated fees.

Varieties of Remortgages

Several types of remortgages cater to different needs, including:

1. Product Transfer: This option allows you to switch to a different mortgage

product with your existing lender. It's often the simplest and most cost-effective way to remortgage.

2. Porting a Mortgage: Porting enables you to move your current mortgage to a new lender. This is a beneficial choice when you're relocating or seeking a better interest rate with a different lender.

3. Equity Release: This type of remortgage permits you to access some of the equity in your home, which can be particularly useful for older homeowners or those requiring funds for various purposes.

Advantages of Remortgaging

Remortgaging offers several potential benefits, such as:

1. Savings: Switching to a lower interest rate through remortgaging can result in significant long-term savings.

2. Altering Mortgage Terms: You can use remortgaging to modify your mortgage terms, including the repayment period or type. This enhances the affordability and flexibility of your mortgage.

3. Equity Release: Remortgaging provides a means to unlock home equity, offering financial opportunities for home improvements or debt consolidation.

Drawbacks of Remortgaging

On the flip side, there are some potential drawbacks to consider, such as:

1. Early Repayment Charges: Remortgaging before your current mortgage term ends may entail

substantial early repayment charges, which should be factored into your decision.

2. Arrangement Fees: Most lenders impose arrangement fees for remortgaging, with varying costs. Comparing these fees from different lenders is crucial.

3. Valuation Fees: To ensure responsible lending, you'll typically need to cover the cost of a home valuation when remortgaging.

Steps for Remortgaging

If you're contemplating remortgaging, here's what you need to do:

1. Shop Around: Compare remortgage offers from different lenders to secure the most favorable deal.

2. Assess Your Needs: Define your remortgage goals, whether it's a

reduced interest rate, adjusted repayment terms, or unlocking equity.

3. Seek Advice: If you're uncertain about the remortgaging process, consider consulting a financial advisor for guidance.

Considerations When Remortgaging

A few key considerations to bear in mind when remortgaging include:

1. Early Repayment Charges: Ensure that you account for any early repayment charges in your decision-making process.

2. Arrangement Fees: Thoroughly assess the arrangement fees applied by different lenders.

3. Valuation Fees: Incorporate the cost of a home valuation into your budget planning for remortgaging.

4. Credit Rating: Your credit rating significantly influences the interest rate offered during remortgaging. A favorable credit rating can lead to a lower interest rate.

5. Income: Your income plays a pivotal role in determining the amount you can borrow for a remortgage. Lenders will assess your ability to manage the monthly repayments based on your income.

In Conclusion

Remortgaging is a valuable strategy for saving money, adjusting mortgage terms, or accessing home equity. Nevertheless, it's essential to carefully evaluate both the advantages and disadvantages before committing to remortgaging. If you're considering remortgaging, consulting a financial advisor is a prudent step to align your decision with your individual financial situation and goals.

Switching to a different mortgage deal

Transitioning to a new mortgage arrangement, often referred to as remortgaging, involves replacing your current mortgage with a fresh one, either from the same lender or a different one. There are various reasons for considering remortgaging, such as:

1. Obtaining a lower interest rate.

2. Modifying the mortgage terms, like adjusting the repayment period or repayment method.

3. Tapping into the equity in your home.

Regarding when you can make this switch, it's typically possible at any time, but early repayment charges (ERCs) may apply, especially if you have a fixed-rate mortgage and are remortgaging before the fixed-rate term ends. These charges vary by lender and mortgage type, so carefully review your current mortgage's terms and conditions before proceeding.

To change to a different mortgage deal, you'll need to compare offers from various lenders to find the most suitable one for your situation. Mortgage comparison websites can help with this process. After selecting a favorable deal, you'll need to apply for the new mortgage and provide information about your income, expenses, and credit history to the lender. Once approved, your new lender will handle paying off your existing mortgage and setting up the new one. This process typically takes a few weeks, so it's wise to plan ahead if you're considering remortgaging.

The advantages of switching to a different mortgage deal include:

1. Potential cost savings, especially if you secure a lower interest rate.
2. Flexibility to adjust the mortgage terms for affordability.
3. The ability to release home equity for various purposes.

However, there are potential drawbacks to consider, such as early repayment charges, arrangement fees imposed by lenders, and the need to pay for a home valuation.

When choosing the right mortgage deal, consider factors like the interest rate, repayment period, repayment type, and associated fees. Careful consideration of your individual needs and circumstances is essential in making an informed decision.

In conclusion, remortgaging can be a valuable strategy to save money, modify mortgage terms, or access home equity. However, thorough evaluation of the pros and cons, as well as comparing offers from different lenders, is crucial before making a decision.

Getting help with mortgage payments

Seeking Assistance with Mortgage Payments

When you encounter difficulties making your mortgage payments, there are several avenues to explore for support. Here's how you can seek help:

1. Initiate a Conversation with Your Lender: When faced with challenges in making mortgage payments, your lender is often the best initial contact. They may present various options, including:

    a. A payment holiday, which offers temporary relief from mortgage payments. These breaks can range from a few months to more extended periods.

    b. A tailored repayment plan designed to suit your unique circumstances. This plan could involve reducing your monthly payments or extending your mortgage term.

    c. Mortgage rescue schemes, specifically designed to aid

homeowners at risk of losing their homes due to unaffordable mortgage payments.

2. Consult a Housing Counselor: Housing counselors can offer free, confidential advice on your mortgage alternatives. They can assist in negotiating with your lender and developing a budget. You can locate a housing counselor in your area through the National Housing Counseling Agencies website.

3. Explore Government Assistance: Several government programs are available to aid homeowners struggling with mortgage payments, including:

   a. The Home Affordable Modification Program (HAMP)

facilitates mortgage modification for increased affordability.

b. The Hardest Hit Fund provides assistance to homeowners in states most affected by the housing crisis.

c. The Homeowner Assistance Fund (HAF) extends aid to homeowners facing financial hardship due to the COVID-19 pandemic.

2. Consider Other Choices: Homeowners with payment difficulties have additional alternatives, including:

a. Refinancing your mortgage: This entails securing a new mortgage to replace the existing one. Refinancing might lead to a lower interest rate, reducing monthly payments.

b. Selling your home: If keeping your home becomes financially unsustainable, selling it could be a viable choice, helping you avoid foreclosure.

In conclusion, if you're struggling to meet your mortgage obligations, don't hesitate to seek assistance. Open a dialogue with your lender promptly and explore the guidance of housing counselors or government support programs. Additional tips for seeking help with mortgage payments include preparing financial documentation, being transparent with your lender, and maintaining patience throughout the negotiation process. Remember, you're not alone; there are resources available to assist homeowners facing mortgage payment challenges.

Chapter 5

Mortgages and financial planning

Impact of Mortgages on Your Finances

Mortgages wield a substantial influence on your financial situation, with both positive and negative consequences. Here's an overview:

Positive Impacts:

1. Homeownership: Mortgages enable you to acquire a valuable asset, your home, which can appreciate in value over time.

2. Building Equity: With each mortgage payment, you accumulate equity, gradually increasing your ownership in your home.

3. Tax Benefits: Homeowners can deduct mortgage interest and property taxes from their federal income taxes, leading to potential savings.

4. Financial Stability: Mortgages provide a structured monthly payment, facilitating financial stability and budgeting.

Negative Impacts:

1. Debt: Mortgages represent a form of debt, necessitating repayment of borrowed funds plus interest over time.

2. Affordability Challenges: Mortgage payments can pose a considerable

financial burden, especially with high-interest rates or short repayment terms.

3. Risk of Foreclosure: Failing to meet mortgage payments can lead to the risk of losing your home through foreclosure.

4. Reduced Flexibility: Having a mortgage can limit your ability to relocate or change jobs, as it requires selling your home or obtaining approval for a new mortgage from another lender.

Overall Impact:

The impact of mortgages on your finances is contingent on your unique circumstances. For some, mortgages serve as a means to build financial security and wealth. However, for others, mortgages can become a financial strain, potentially causing stress and financial hardship.

Minimizing Negative Impacts:

To mitigate the adverse effects of mortgages, consider the following strategies:

- Pre-Approval: Get pre-approved for a mortgage to determine your borrowing capacity and monthly payments.

- Larger Down Payment: A substantial down payment reduces monthly obligations and minimizes the risk of owning more than your home's value.

- Shorter Repayment Term: Opting for a shorter term increases monthly payments but reduces overall interest costs.

- Mortgage Insurance: Consider mortgage insurance to safeguard against foreclosure if you encounter payment difficulties.

Choosing the appropriate mortgage insurance depends on your financial circumstances, risk factors, and your family's needs. Consulting a financial advisor for personalized advice is advisable.

Protecting Your Mortgage with Insurance:

Several types of mortgage insurance can provide protection:

1. Private Mortgage Insurance (PMI): Required for down payments under 20%, it safeguards the lender if you default. Once you reach 20% equity, you can cancel PMI.

2. Mortgage Protection Insurance (MPI): Protects against job loss,

disability, or death, covering payments for a set period.

3. Mortgage Life Insurance: Pays off your mortgage balance upon your death, relieving your family from a financial burden.

Selecting the right mortgage insurance hinges on your unique requirements and considerations. Consulting a financial advisor can aid in making an informed choice.

To safeguard your mortgage and home, follow these tips:

- Get pre-approved to determine your borrowing capacity.
- Consider a larger down payment for reduced monthly obligations.
- Evaluate the advantages of a shorter repayment term.

- Explore mortgage insurance options to protect against unforeseen circumstances.

Planning for retirement with a mortgage

Planning for retirement while still having a mortgage can be a challenging endeavor, but remember, you're not alone. Many individuals face this situation, and there are strategies to simplify the process.

One distinctive perspective to consider is that your mortgage can serve as an asset during retirement. With a mortgage fully paid off, you'll possess substantial home equity that can be leveraged for income, handling unexpected expenses, or ensuring financial peace of mind.

For those who haven't paid off their mortgage upon retirement, there are options to make it more manageable. Downsizing to a smaller home can reduce monthly expenses, as can refinancing to extend the mortgage term, although this might result in paying more interest over time.

If meeting mortgage payments in retirement becomes challenging, numerous government and nonprofit programs, like the Home Equity Conversion Mortgage (HECM) program, can provide assistance. HECM enables homeowners aged 62 and older to borrow against home equity without making monthly payments, with repayment occurring upon selling the home or the homeowner's passing.

Regardless of your situation, there are various approaches to plan for retirement with a mortgage. Initiating a side hustle, such as freelancing or selling products online, is a noteworthy tip to generate extra income, increase financial flexibility, and stay engaged in retirement.

Transferring your mortgage debt to your heirs is also a consideration.

When you pass away, your estate assumes responsibility for paying off the mortgage using your assets. To facilitate this transfer, you can opt for joint tenancy or tenancy in common, but it's essential to assess your heirs' financial capacity and preferences. Additionally, reviewing your will with an attorney to ensure a clear distribution plan is advisable.

When transferring your mortgage to heirs, be aware of tax implications, including the step-up in basis, which adjusts the property's value upon inheritance, potentially reducing capital gains tax, and the mortgage interest deduction that heirs may qualify for on their federal tax returns. In conclusion, passing on your mortgage to your heirs can be a beneficial way to help them inherit your home and prevent foreclosure. Nevertheless, thorough consideration of your heirs' financial situation, preferences, and tax implications is vital before making a decision.

Additional tips for passing on your mortgage to your heirs:

1. Consult with your lender to explore available options. Some lenders

might offer specialized programs tailored to heirs inheriting a mortgage.

2. Prior to inheriting the home, consider obtaining pre-approval for a mortgage. This will provide insights into how much you can borrow and the associated monthly payments.

3. Ponder the idea of purchasing mortgage insurance, as it can serve as a safeguard against foreclosure if your heirs encounter difficulties making mortgage payments.

4. Develop a budget and adhere to it. This proactive approach will assist in managing mortgage payments and the various expenses associated with homeownership.

By adhering to these recommendations, you can facilitate a seamless and successful transition for your heirs as they take ownership of your home.

Obtaining Financial Guidance for Mortgages

Securing financial guidance for mortgages is a prudent strategy to ensure you make informed decisions that align with your unique requirements. Numerous avenues are available to seek such advice, including:

1. Consulting a Mortgage Broker: Mortgage brokers, licensed professionals, can assist in comparing mortgage options from various lenders to identify the most suitable choice. Typically, mortgage brokers are compensated by lenders, making their services cost-free for consumers.

2. Engaging a Financial Advisor: A financial advisor, another licensed expert, can offer comprehensive financial planning assistance, including guidance on mortgages. Using their services usually involves certain charges.

3. Seeking Guidance from a Housing Counselor: Housing counselors, nonprofit professionals, deliver impartial and complimentary advice on mortgages. The National Housing Counseling Agency's website can help you locate a housing counselor in your area.

Key Questions to Ask When Seeking Financial Advice on Mortgages:

1. What mortgage options are available to me?

2. Which mortgage aligns with my financial situation?

3. What is the interest rate associated with the mortgage?

4. What are the monthly payment requirements?

5. Are there any fees linked to the mortgage?

6. Is there a prepayment penalty?

7. What are the risks associated with obtaining a mortgage?

Selecting a Financial Advisor for Mortgage Guidance:

When choosing a financial advisor for mortgage-related advice, consider the following factors:

1. **Experience**: Verify that the financial advisor possesses

experience in dealing with mortgages.

2. **Credentials**: Ensure the financial advisor is licensed and holds appropriate credentials.

3. **Fees**: Inquire about the financial advisor's fee structure upfront.

4. **Reputation**: Solicit information about the financial advisor's reputation and request references from previous clients.

In Conclusion:

Obtaining financial advice for mortgages is a wise step to make informed choices that align with your specific needs. Since multiple avenues are available to access such guidance, it's advisable to explore different options and select an advisor with whom you feel comfortable.

Here are additional tips for acquiring financial advice on mortgages:

1. Be ready to furnish the financial advisor with details about your financial status, including income, expenses, and outstanding debts.

2. Be transparent with the financial advisor regarding your financial goals and objectives.

3. Don't hesitate to pose questions and engage in negotiation when necessary.

4. Insist on having all agreements and terms in writing before signing any documents.

By following these guidelines, you can optimize your experience with financial advice and secure the most suitable mortgage for your requirements.

Conclusion

Mortgages and interest rates are two of the most important factors to consider when buying a home. The type of mortgage you choose and the interest rate you get will have a significant impact on your monthly payments and the total amount of interest you pay over the life of the loan.

It is important to compare mortgage products from different lenders and to shop around for the best interest rate. You should also consider your individual needs and circumstances when choosing a mortgage. For example, if you need to keep your monthly payments low, you may want to consider an interest-only mortgage. However, it is important to remember that interest-only mortgages can be riskier than other types of mortgages because you will be responsible for repaying the entire principal amount of the loan at the end of the interest-only period.

If you are unsure which type of mortgage is right for you or what interest rate you should be getting, it is important to seek professional advice from a qualified mortgage advisor. They can help you compare different mortgage products and find the best deal for your needs.